DEAR DAD,

THANK YOU FOR
BEING MINE

To Pop

With love from Edith

12/94

DEAR DAD,

THANK YOU FOR BEING MINE

Scott Matthews
Tamara Nikuradse

 BANTAM BOOKS New York Toronto London Sydney Auckland

DEAR DAD, THANK YOU FOR BEING MINE

A Bantam Book / June 1993

All rights reserved.
Copyright © 1993 by Scott Matthews and Tamara Nikuradse.
Book design by Ellen Cipriano
No part of this book may be reproduced or transmitted in any form or
by any means, electronic or mechanical, including photocopying, recording, or
by any information storage and retrieval system, without permission in writing from the publisher.
For information address: Bantam Books.

Library of Congress Cataloging-in-Publication Data

Matthews, Scott.
    Dear Dad, thank you for being mine / by Scott Matthews, Tamara
Nikuradse.
        p.   cm.
    ISBN 0-553-37198-3
    1. Father and child—Miscellanea.   2. Gratitude—Miscellanea.
I. Nikuradse, Tamara.   II. Title.
HQ756.M36   1993
306.874'2—dc20   92-40270
                                                                   CIP

Published simultaneously in the United States and Canada

PRINTED IN THE UNITED STATES OF AMERICA

FFG   0 9 8 7 6 5 4

*Dedicated to all Dads who
make these thank-yous possible*

Acknowledgments

Thank you to our parents, Glenn and Gail Matthews and Charles and Odeline Townes, for the inspiration to write this book.

Thank you to our friends who helped make this book possible: Len Berardis, Susan and Michael Caplan, Evelyn Fazio, Joline Godfrey, Sheila Kenyon, Brett and Ginger Matthews, Becky and Rachel Salmon, Tanya Townes, Connie Patsalos and Cheryl Wells (for the jump start), and the three coauthors of our first book, *Stuck in the Seventies*, Jay Kerness, Jay Steele, and Greg White.

Thank you, Mary Jane Ross, our agent, for your diligence and guidance.

Thank you, Barbara Alpert, our friend and editor, for your enthusiasm, encouragement, and editing prowess. Thank you, Matthew Shear, for your confidence. And thank you to all of Scott's friends and colleagues at Bantam who brought this book to you.

Thank you.

Scott and Tamara

Introduction

During a recent move, we came across a box full of family pictures. You know the ones. Pictures celebrating first potties and first steps, first dances and first dates. Pictures of bare baby bottoms on fur rugs and geeky grins found only in high school yearbooks.

With each picture the memories started to flood, and they reminded us of all the things that our parents have given to us—material and immaterial—things that we still carry with us to this day, things that made us who we are today. The pictures also reminded us of the many times that we forgot to thank our parents, especially for the little things that we had taken for granted. Deciding that it was never too late, we started compiling our thank-yous to present to our parents as long-overdue gifts. We hope they spark memories from your past that hold special meanings for you.

We know that every child has some special thank-yous to say to his or her parents, so we left room for you to add your own thoughts at the end. Of course, feel free to edit anything in here to make it fit your father perfectly.

DEAR DAD,

THANK YOU...

Thank you for creating me with love.

Thank you for running out to find an anchovy-and-dill-pickle hot fudge sundae at one in the morning to satisfy my cravings.

Thank you for getting Mom and me to
the delivery room safe and
(almost) sound.

Thank you for not fainting upon
hearing of my arrival.

Thank you for saying my birth was the
greatest day of your life.

Thank you for passing out bubble-gum cigars when I was born.

Thank you for studying Dr. Spock.

Thank you for shooting lots of baby pictures.

Thank you for cradling me in your arms.

Thank you for not dropping me on my head when I was little.

Thank you for hanging the bobbing clown-head mobile above my crib to amuse me while I lay on my back with nothing to do for most of that first year.

Thank you for pushing my carriage.

Thank you for not throwing me out with the bath water.

Thank you for loving me no matter
how goofy I looked.

Thank you for not agreeing when your
friends said I looked liked E.T.

Thank you for never forgetting
to feed me.

Thank you for picking up my spoon or bowl twelve times per feeding.

Thank you for coaxing the tunnel to open by going "Choo-choo-choo."

Thank you for cleaning up the mess when the choo-choo train backed up and spit up all over you.

Thank you for conversing with me in my native language, baby talk, until I became bilingual and could speak Adult.

Thank you for saying "Dada . . . Dada . . . Dada" one zillion times until I finally caught on.

Thank you for changing my diapers as soon as you noticed I was soggy, instead of calling Mom.

Thank you for explaining the difference
between "number one" and
"number two."

Thank you for responding to my early-
morning cries in 5.3 seconds flat.

Thank you for holding a press
conference when I took my first steps.

Thank you for playing This Little Piggy
with my little piggies.

Thank you for buying me my very own
car seat.

Thank you for pulling the worms out of
my mouth when we went fishing.

Thank you for hiding my boo-boos
behind a Band-Aid®.

Thank you for dead-bolting the bottom
cabinets and child-proofing the
electrical outlets.

Thank you for tugging my finger from
my nose.

Thank you for trying to explain where the birdie and cheese were when the big hairy guy at the department store tried to get me to smile for a picture.

Thank you for reading *Little Red Riding Hood* for nineteen straight nights.

Thank you for marking each quarter inch I grew on the door frame.

Thank you for keeping your cool through my terrible twos, and my thoroughly exhausting threes, and my fearsome fours, and . . .

Thank you for telling me once-upon-a-time stories.

Thank you for the stern lecture when I forgot to look both ways before crossing the street.

Thank you for crawling on your hands and knees to show me how to escape from the house in case of a fire.

Thank you for jogging my memory by writing an "L" on one sneaker and an "R" on the other.

Thank you for escorting me into public rest rooms.

Thank you for my nicknames.

Thank you for making me sit six feet from the color TV.

Thank you for explaining why the Coyote chased the Road Runner and how Yosemite Sam lived after being shot by a cannonball.

Thank you for warning me to keep my fingers away from door edges.

Thank you for discreetly stopping me before I asked the baby-sitter if I could connect the dots on her face.

Thank you for treating me to Walt Disney movies.

Thank you for teaching me to "just say no" to candy from strangers and, later, to drugs.

Thank you for making me wash the sludge from behind my ears.

Thank you for not getting too angry when you found the melted ice pop in my jacket pocket.

Thank you for filling my piggy bank with your spare change and letting me stick the knife into Porky's back to retrieve a few coins in emergencies.

Thank you for reminding me not to start eating until Mom sat down.

Thank you for not swatting me when I asked you if you'd lived with the cavemen.

Thank you for helping me make all sides of the Rubik's Cube the same color.

Thank you for listening to me sing
"The Alphabet Song" over and
over again.

Thank you for always laughing at my
jokes, no matter how bad they were.

Thank you for wasting electricity to
keep my night-light on through the
night so that the bogey monster
stayed away.

Thank you for holding my hand when we walked down the street.

Thank you for not letting me know what was going on behind your locked bedroom door.

Thank you for telling me to mind my P's and Q's.

Thank you for launching a search party to find me when you lost me in the department store.

Thank you for finding me in the toy department.

Thank you for buying me a toy because you felt guilty for losing me and you didn't want me to tell Mom.

Thank you for launching a search party to find me when you lost me again in the department store.

Thank you for finding me in the candy aisle. . . .

Thank you for making me "go" just minutes before we left for a long car ride.

Thank you for pulling to the side of the road when I *had* to go twenty minutes later.

Thank you for singing "Ninety-nine Bottles of Beer on the Wall" during our road trips.

Thank you for always answering my
"Are we there yet?"

Thank you for listening to my favorite
radio station even though it gave you a
headache.

Thank you for giving me money to ride
the mechanical horse.

Thank you for telling me "That's the way the cookie crumbles" when you caught me with my hand in the cookie jar and my body tipping precariously off a chair.

Thank you for taking me to see the clowns in the circus.

Thank you for urging me to be a leader and not a follower.

Thank you for rescuing my tongue from the frozen metal ice tray when I licked it on a double dare.

Thank you for rescuing my tongue from the frozen metal ice tray when I licked it on a triple dare.

Thank you for telling all of your friends that I was a child prodigy.

Thank you for saving a tabby cat from the animal shelter and allowing me to name her Dog Meat.

Thank you for rescuing Dog Meat before I turned the knob to the spin cycle.

Thank you for not giving me something to cry about despite your warnings.

Thank you for never dropping me off at the orphanage or selling me to the circus.

Thank you for never telling me to go outside and play in the traffic.

Thank you for teaching me not to roll with the punches—especially when someone was giving me a black eye.

Thank you for letting me put the money in the meter and turn the knob.

Thank you for not letting me spend my hard-earned allowance on sea monkeys, X-ray glasses, or any of the other gimmicky gadgets advertised on the back pages of my comic books.

Thank you for reminding me that "Hey" is for horses.

Thank you for grabbing the plunger when we couldn't get the frog out of the toilet.

Thank you for immortalizing my embarrassment with a photo of me... *no*... it's too embarrassing even to write about it!

Thanks a lot for showing that photo to everyone when you got the chance.

Thank you for trying to explain why G.I. Joe shouldn't sleep in Barbie's bed.

Thank you for teaching me which coins equal one dollar.

Thank you for not letting me stunt my growth by drinking coffee.

Thank you for showing me
how to whistle.

Thank you for removing the splinter
from my finger and keeping the blood
loss to under a pint.

Thank you for stopping me before I
broke the bed by playing trampoline.

Thank you for warning me not to tease German shepherds behind low picket fences.

Thank you for letting me interrupt you—occasionally—when your favorite TV shows were on.

Thank you for packing up pillows and blankets and taking us to the drive-in theater.

Thank you for creating convincing excuses when I overheard you and Mom fighting.

Thank you for taking me shopping (and paying) for Mom's Mother's Day and birthday gifts.

Thank you for pretending you liked the ties that I got you as gifts and for wearing them only on "very special" occasions.

Thank you for saying "Finders keepers, losers weepers" when I found coins in the couch that Grandpa always sat in.

Thank you for making pitchers of Kool-Aid on hot summer days.

Thank you for taking me on camping and fishing trips.

Thank you for baiting my hook with a plump worm and cheering when I caught a big one.

Thank you for figuring out how to stop the leaks in the tent when it rained.

Thank you for teaching me an ancient Indian trick to build the perfect campfire (lighter fluid and a match).

Thank you for telling me wicked scary
ghost stories around the campfire.

Thank you for making "s'mores" over
our campfire by melting marshmallows
and placing the gooey mess on a hunk
of chocolate between two
graham crackers.

Thank you for spending your summer
weekends constructing a two-room
tree fort.

Thank you for taking me to the
ballpark for a baseball game and buying
me two dogs, a packet of peanuts, two
popcorns, three ice creams, and a Coke.

Thank you for introducing me to "Plop,
plop, fizz, fizz."

Thank you for buying me a Schwinn bike with a yellow banana seat and wicked cool streamers flowing from the handlebars.

Thank you for holding on to my bicycle seat and running at my side for six whole blocks the day you took off my training wheels.

Thank you for never jumping off the other end of the seesaw.

Thank you for building sand castles with me and for being a good sport when I buried you from neck to toe in the sand.

Thank you for bodysurfing with me.

Thank you for letting me ride on your shoulders when we watched parades.

Thank you for prying me from your leg and forcing me to attend my first day of school.

Thank you for living near school so I didn't have to walk up a twelve-mile-long hill against forty-knot winds in a raging blizzard to get to school by seven in the morning so that I could shovel coal into the belly of the school's furnace so that the classroom would be above freezing by noon—like you had to.

Thank you for always listening to my schoolyard tall tales.

Thank you for being a great Papa Bear and protecting your cub by calling Mr. Dudley to tell him that his little "Milk Dud" was stealing my lunch money, and if little Milk Dud didn't stop, you'd come over and punch Mr. Dudley in the nose.

Thank you for practicing the Pledge of Allegiance and "The Star-Spangled Banner" with me.

Thank you for buying me new eyeglasses when I lost them.

Thank you for buying me newer eyeglasses when I lost them again.

Thank you for reassuring me when my I.Q. scores indicated that I wasn't a genius.

Thank you for drilling me on my spelling words.

Thank you for attending Parent-Teacher Nights and telling me all the good things that my teachers had to say about me.

Thank you for helping me with my
science projects.

Thank you for listening to me practice
the scales on my musical instrument
over and over and over again.

Thank you for showing me how long
division worked and explaining it over a
thousand times until I finally caught on.

Thank you for making me feel better when I didn't get the starring role as the mushroom in my third-grade play.

Thank you for not snoring during my debut performance as a pea pod.

Thank you for applauding even when I missed my one and only line.

Thank you for curing my hiccups.

Thank you for showing me that Dads do housework as well as Moms . . . when the spirit moved you.

Thank you for making me count to ten before I exploded.

Thank you for cooking Oscar Mayer wieners for my lunch when you heard me sing "Oh, I wish I were an . . ."

Thank you for climbing the tree to free my kite after you got it stuck.

Thank you for telling me that a little work never hurt anyone.

Thank you for reminding me that a cluttered room equals a cluttered mind.

Thank you for raking the leaves into a humongous pile so I could jump into it.

Thank you for dressing up like a goblin on Halloween and trying to scare my friends.

Thank you for escorting your Casper the Friendly Ghost around the neighborhood trick-or-treating.

Thank you for taking only one out of every five candies as a "Daddy Tummy Tax."

Thank you for letting me carve a portion of the Thanksgiving turkey.

Thank you for explaining what a yam was.

Thank you for lobbing the first snowball to start the battle.

Thank you for not getting too angry when I used your favorite hat to top the head of my five-foot snowman.

Thank you for waxing my toboggan.

Thank you for teaching me to ice-skate.

Thank you for letting me ski between your legs down the "advanced" slope after I insisted I could do it all by myself.

Thank you for following my tracks into the woods and disentangling my skis from the bushes.

Thank you for having hot chocolate with marshmallows waiting for me after I came in from the cold.

Thank you for drying out my soggy and cold body.

Thank you for creating magic
during the holidays.

Thank you for making sure we received the *Sears Wish Book.*

Thank you for holding me up so that I could place the star on the top of the tree after we trimmed it.

Thank you for letting me light the holiday candles that made our living room glow.

Thank you for believing my fibs when you caught me peeking at the gifts.

Thank you for mailing my letters to the North Pole.

Thank you for telling me that the blinking red light flying in the sky was Rudolph's flashing red nose.

Thank you for drinking the milk and
eating the cookies that I left out
for Santa.

Thank you for staying up half the night
on Christmas Eve trying to translate the
unreadable instructions and assemble my
toys before I woke up at five in the
morning and dragged you out of bed.

Thank you for encouraging me to share my possessions—especially all the toys I'd just received.

Thank you for wrapping up my puppy, Toto, and placing the wiggling box under the tree.

Thank you for filling a bowl with my dinner, placing it on the floor, and letting me eat with my puppy.

Thank you for walking Toto—all the times that I forgot.

Thank you for eating the hard-boiled eggs that I colored for Easter.

Thank you for allowing me to sleep over at my friend's house.

Thank you for telling me once.

Thank you for telling me
a thousand times.

Thank you for not keeping me in your
"dog house" for more than a day.

Thank you for insisting that I always
buckle up in the car.

Thank you for making fresh lemonade
for my sidewalk stand.

Thank you for buying five glasses of my
warm lemonade and for treating all of
the neighbors who passed by.

Thank you for explaining why Jaws, my goldfish, was doing the backstroke.

Thank you for scooping Jaws from the tank, saying a few kind words about him, and burying him in the porcelain sea.

Thank you for letting Toto rest at my feet under the dinner table on tuna surprise casserole nights.

Thank you for taking me to McDonald's so that I could order "two all-beef patties special sauce lettuce cheese pickles onions on a sesame seed bun—bun seed sesame a on onions pickles cheese lettuce sauce special patties beef-all two."

Thank you for buying a dozen assorted donuts and the Sunday papers every weekend.

Thank you for letting me read the Sunday comics before you.

Thank you for making me drink a glass of pickle juice to teach me a lesson after you caught my dirty hand in the pickle jar.

Thank you for telling me that Dog Meat ran away instead of what the delivery truck's tire really did.

Thank you for not being a "Daddy Dearest."

Thank you for being (mostly) all bark and no bite.

Thank you for telling me "One day you'll thank me for this." Today's the day . . . Thank you for that.

Thank you for buying batteries
for my toys.

Thank you for setting my digital watch
to the correct time and
teaching me how.

Thank you for asking for the time.

Thank you for buying Hostess Twinkies
so that I could suck out the
creme fillings.

Thank you for letting me spy on the grown-ups during the neighborhood block parties.

Thank you for letting me cry and for never telling me "Don't be a sissy."

Thank you for seizing the lawn darts when you caught me playing chicken with my friends.

Thank you for teaching me to care for the environment before it became the right thing to do.

Thank you for looking the other way when Grammy spoiled me.

Thank you for showing me that my infrequent spankings hurt you a lot more than me.

Thank you for passing through your leisure suit phase—quickly.

Thank you for having the people at the office save their letters from foreign lands so that I could add the stamps to my collection.

Thank you for knowing that I never meant it when I said "I wish I was never born!" or "I wish you weren't my father!"

Thank you for strapping a Styrofoam bomb to my back, taking me to a pool, and teaching me to swim.

Thank you for subscribing to cable TV.

Thank you for letting me stay up late—sometimes—to watch those crazy late-night shows.

Thank you for photocopying my club's bylaws and initiation forms at your office.

Thank you for not looking up my strange words in the dictionary when we played Scrabble.

Thank you for correcting my *gottas* and *donchas*.

Thank you for showing me how to make do with what I had.

Thank you for pointing out the Big and Little Dippers and the North Star.

Thank you for figuring out how to eject the eight-track tape from the player when it got stuck.

Thank you for buying me a calculator.

Thank you for introducing me to the dictionary, *Roget's Thesaurus*, and the encyclopedia.

Thank you for teaching me self-reliance when I asked a question by telling me I could look it up.

Thank you for teaching me how to defend myself.

Thank you for making me wash my hands before I touched food—with hot water and soap.

Thank you for making me rewash my hands when I didn't pass the inspection.

Thank you for always being
my friend.

Thank you for laughing with me.

Thank you for wishing and wanting only the best for me.

Thank you for reminding me that good losers are the winners and bad winners are the losers.

Thank you for not admonishing me when I wiped my face after Aunt Gertrude succeeded in giving me a slushy surprise kiss.

Thank you for encouraging me to bang nails for you when you built something.

Thank you for explaining the function of a three-quarter drill head bit as opposed to a two-bit drill head bit.

Thank you for treating me to a large Baskin-Robbins hot fudge sundae when I least expected it.

Thank you for keeping your promises and expecting me to do the same.

Thank you for driving me to the ninety-nine-cent matinee on rainy Saturdays.

Thank you for buying me my very own
pizza with my favorite toppings.

Thank you for finally breaking down
and purchasing a turntable adapter so I
could play my 45s on your stereo.

Thank you for showing me why
discipline is important.

Thank you for teaching me about the birds and the bees.

Thank you for hiding *The Joy of Sex* where I could find it to help me fill in some of the details you left out.

Thank you for escorting me to a tree to demonstrate that money doesn't grow on it.

Thank you for letting me talk on your CB radio with my own handle.

Thank you for figuring out how to clean my Crazy Straw after I drank chocolate milk.

Thank you for showing me how to lip-synch the words to the hymns in church.

Thank you for reassuring me that I can be whatever I want to be.

Thank you for saying "I love you."

Thank you for looking into my eyes when we spoke and for expecting me to do the same.

Thank you for squeezing the blood out of my hand with your firm handshake and expecting me to do the same.

Thank you for opening up a blue book savings account and for helping me make my first deposit.

Thank you for barging into the room to break up the spin-the-bottle game before it was my turn.

Thank you for helping me construct a family tree.

Thank you for playing catch with me in the backyard.

Thank you for sitting in the stands in the pouring rain to watch me warm the bench.

Thank you for the cheers that I heard when I was on the field.

Thank you for pinch-hitting in our front-yard Wiffle Ball games.

Thank you for nailing the sign "Growing Kids, Not Grass" to the tree in the front yard when a neighbor complained that our deteriorating front lawn decreased the neighborhood's property values.

Thank you for letting my sports schedules take precedence over your other plans.

Thank you for sitting in the hot sun and watching the ball go through your little ball player's legs at third base.

Thank you for chewing out old Mr. Tortellini when he yelled from the bleachers, "Take that bum out at third!"

Thank you for restraining Mom and telling old Mr. Tortellini that you don't care if I'm a Yogi Berra or a Bob Uecker, you're proud of me.

Thank you for my first name. I always liked it.

Thank you for allowing me to shadow you for a day at your office.

Thank you for telling me "Ask your mother" when you didn't want to say no, thus increasing my odds for success.

Thank you for pulling an Emily Post by instructing me—night after night—to keep my elbows off the table, to stop slurping my soup, to place my napkin in my lap, to stop slouching in my chair, and never to burp in public.

Thank you for not forcing me to eat
brussels sprouts.

Thank you for always giving me your
very best and expecting the same
in return.

Thank you for driving me around my
paper route.

Thank you for doing my paper route
when I had a cold.

Thank you for letting me hang out at the mall with my friends.

Thank you for warning me to never pass wind in a crowded elevator again, especially when we have another ten floors to travel.

Thank you for forcing me to deposit all of my birthday checks into a savings account so that I would have a little nest egg when I turned eighteen.

Thank you for inspiring me to follow my dreams.

Thank you for taking me with you on vacations.

Thank you for working days, and sometimes nights, to put food on the table and a roof over my head and clothes on my back.

Thank you for telling me when it was time to start using deodorant and mouthwash.

Thank you for making me fess up to my mistakes.

Thank you for admitting that you don't know the origin of the universe.

Thank you for putting up with my
teenage mood swings.

Thank you for tolerating me during my
Woodstock phase.

Thank you for tolerating me during my
rock 'n' roll phase.

Thank you for tolerating me during my
blast-the-stereo-and-blow-the-
speaker phase.

Thank you for tolerating me during my hogging-the-phone phase.

Thank you for tolerating me during my get-rich-quick phase.

Thank you for understanding me during my dark-and-brooding, chip-on-my-shoulder, life's-not-fair, antiestablishment phase.

Thank you for not grounding me for the *entire* summer after I came home with three beers in my stomach and three more on your shag carpeting in the den.

Thank you for not getting too mad when the vice principal called.

Thank you for letting me know how much I had hurt you when you caught me in a lie.

Thank you for trusting me again.

Thank you for not quitting on me.

Thank you for making sure I knew
when I was testing your limits.

Thank you for trying to close the
generation gap.

Thank you for insisting on seeing my report card.

Thank you for rewarding my As and Bs with praise.

Thank you for rewarding my Cs with "You can do better."

Thank you for rewarding my Ds and Fs with "You #$%& well better do better!"

Thank you for not expecting me
to be perfect.

Thank you for debating with me at the dinner table to help me hone that skill.

Thank you for teaching me the concept of K.I.S.S.—Keep It Simple, Stupid.

Thank you for encouraging me to read about the world news in the daily paper.

Thank you for telling me that honesty isn't the best policy—it's the *only* policy!

Thank you for letting me have a first date before I was married.

Thank you for not chaperoning me on my first date.

Thank you for pretending you didn't know me when I ran into a pack of friends at the mall.

Thank you for preparing a great breakfast with plenty of "brain food" the morning of my SATs.

Thank you for waiting for me to return home from school so that I could open the envelope and be the first to see my SAT scores.

Thank you for not being disappointed when I didn't score 1600 on my SATs.

Thank you for purchasing a VCR.

Thank you for taking my phone calls at work no matter how busy you were.

Thank you for always listening to me.

Thank you for giving me the benefit of the doubt.

Thank you for teaching me how to tip those who deserve it.

Thank you for shooting hoops with me until after dark.

Thank you for helping me get my driver's license by letting me practice with you in the car.

Thank you for accepting the destruction of your whitewall tires while teaching me to parallel park.

Thank you for teaching me to jump-start a car and to change a flat tire.

Thank you for warning me about picking up hitchhikers.

Thank you for not putting me in traction when you found that little scratch—okay, okay, dent—in your car.

Thank you for paying the skyrocketing
car insurance bills.

Thank you for making sure that I
always had money in my pocket when I
went out with my friends in case
I needed to call you.

Thank you for keeping the back door
open and the front light on when
I came home later than you could stay up.

Thank you for helping me with my taxes on April 15 at 11:37 P.M.

Thank you for not telling Mom about you-know-what.

Thank you for appreciating my taste in "noise" and for introducing me to your generation's "music."

Thank you for teaching me how to balance my checkbook.

Thank you for teaching me to be suspicious of the words "The check is in the mail."

Thank you for loaning me money and insisting that I pay you back with interest.

Thank you for believing me when I told you that "the check is in the mail."

Thank you for making me take responsibility for my actions.

Thank you for taking two dozen Polaroids as I tried to escape the house with my prom date.

Thank you for proofreading my college applications.

Thank you for wearing one of my Father's Day ties to my high school graduation.

Thank you for my special high school graduation gift.

Thank you for preparing me for college.

Thank you for packing up my room at home, transporting the boxes to college, and carrying them up five flights of stairs (in ninety-degree weather) to my dorm room—back and forth—eight times over the course of four years.

Thank you for not hiding your tears and for telling me that you'd miss me.

Thank you for enrolling me in the American Automobile Association just in case.

Thank you for scrimping on the household budget for many, many years to pay my college tuition.

Thank you for attending Parents' Weekends and taking some of my friends out to dinner.

Thank you for encouraging me to seek campus jobs to earn my spending money.

Thank you for not forcing a college major down my throat and letting me decide for myself.

Thank you for insisting on seeing my college report cards.

Thank you for allowing me to study abroad for a semester.

Thank you for accepting my collect phone calls.

Thank you for inviting some friends who couldn't afford to travel home to spend Thanksgiving with us and making it special.

Thank you for allowing me to spend a summer at school to wait on tables and spend time with my friends, well, one *special* friend in particular . . . who happened to answer the phone every time you called me.

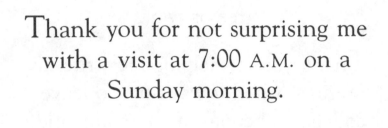

Thank you for not surprising me with a visit at 7:00 A.M. on a Sunday morning.

Thank you for letting me spread my wings to fly—even though I flew into a tree or two.

Thank you for helping me write my résumé when it was time to leave college and confront the real world.

Thank you for stressing the importance of having no typos in my résumé.

Thank you for buying me my first *real* business suit for my interviews.

Thank you for your help during the entire job-hunting expedition and for your serious career advice.

Thank you for telling your friends that I'd be "quite an asset" at their company.

Thank you for not nagging me to accept a job offer from a company that I didn't want to work for.

Thank you for attending my college graduation.

Thank you for wearing one of my Father's Day ties to my college graduation.

Thank you for giving me some of your furniture from the house when I got a place of my own.

Thank you for missing me so much but letting me go.

Thank you for setting me up on some blind dates, but not expecting too much.

Thank you for teaching me that a penny saved is not really a penny earned after you calculate the impact of inflation and taxes.

Thank you for showing me how to boil a live crustacean humanely.

Thank you for handing down your top-secret barbecue-sauce recipe.

Thank you for encouraging me to reach for my goals.

Thank you for grounding me with a strong sense of reality.

Thank you for reminding me that few shortcuts exist in life.

Thank you for almost never lying to me—well, except for one or two little fibs that I will remember when I have kids.

Thank you for teaching me that a contract is only as good as the person signing it.

Thank you for appreciating all of me.

Thank you for reminding me that life can be cruel and unfair for no reason at all, but that *I* have no excuse to be cruel and unfair.

Thank you for telling me not to cry over spilt milk (unless the cow fell on me).

Thank you for my common sense.

Thank you for stating that it is "better to light a candle than curse the darkness" . . . or better yet, to pay the electricity bill.

Thank you for teaching me to give credit where credit is due.

Thank you for requiring me to perform "bread labor" around the house and yard when I came home to spend some time.

Thank you for teaching me how to build a perfect fire in the fireplace with real logs instead of sawdust logs.

Thank you for instilling in me a strong sense of self-reliance.

Thank you for encouraging me to seek alternatives to problems and to weigh those alternatives to find the solutions.

Thank you for not trying to keep up with the Joneses.

Thank you for teaching me about the hazards of fine print.

Thank you for believing that all people are created equal regardless of gender, race, creed, origin, or sexual preference.

Thank you for reminding me that winners never quit and quitters never win.

Thank you for teaching me "to thine own self be true."

Thank you for always being there
when I needed you.

Thank you for giving me a healthy dose of skepticism when confronted with claims from advertisers, politicians, lawyers, and car salespeople.

Thank you for showing me how to march to the beat of a different drummer on a road less traveled.

Thank you for telling me all your best homespun clichés (the ones I thought you had created before I read one of those best-selling little books about life and such), like . . .

. . . *Unless you paddle your own canoe, you won't move.*

. . . *When life gives you lemons, make lemonade.*

. . . *No pain, no strain, no gain.*

Thank you for cultivating my sense of humor.

Thank you for teaching me about my roots.

Thank you for stressing that it is important to strive for my goals.

Thank you for teaching me that life does not come with money-back guarantees and warranties.

Thank you for reminding me not to judge a book by its cover.

Thank you for encouraging me to live my own dreams rather than someone else's.

Thank you for teaching me that nothing ever comes easy and that you have to work *very hard* to realize your goals.

Thank you for sharing with me the
mistakes that you made so that I can try
to avoid them.

Thank you for defining altruism,
integrity, perseverance, and loyalty by
your example.

Thank you for living by the
Ten Commandments.

Thank you for showing me how to thank God.

Thank you for our "family values."

Thank you for passing on to me our family's greatest and most valuable asset . . . our reputation.

Thank you for being my hero.

Thank you for a great childhood.

Thank you for preparing me for adulthood.

Thank you for giving me the best years of your life.

Thank you for your sacrifices.

Thank you for showing me how to
express my love.

Thank you for being you.

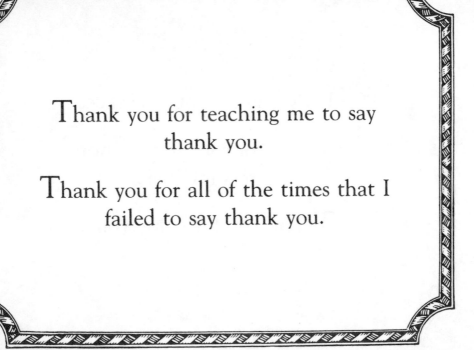

Thank you for teaching me to say thank you.

Thank you for all of the times that I failed to say thank you.

Thank you for your love.

Thank you with all of my
heart and soul.

Thank you for being mine.

And most of all, thank you for
being the best Dad in the universe!

Special Thank-Yous Just for My Dad

Thank you <u>Warming up the car in Winter.</u>

Thank you <u>eating my 4H food & saying</u>
it was good.

Thank you <u>putting up with projects</u>
all over the house.

Thank you <u>believing in me.</u>

... going to church with the
family.

... looking at the stars on a cool, clear night.

Thank you _driving a long way to visit me in the hospital._

Thank you _for the secure feeling that your mom would never need a divorce_

Thank you _sending me through college_

Thank you _making me work in the garden even when I complained._

Thank you _for loving me._

ABOUT THE AUTHORS

Scott is the son of Glenn and Gail Matthews.
Tamara is the daughter of Charles and Odeline
Townes and Alexander Nikuradse.

If you have a special thank-you for your Dad that
you'd like to share, please send it to:

Scott Matthews and Tamara Nikuradse
Bantam Books
1540 Broadway
New York, NY 10036

Please include your name and address so that we can
give you credit if we include it in future editions.
Thank you.

DON'T FORGET... EVERY DAY IS MOTHER'S DAY.

Dear Mom,

- Thank you for letting me run away from home and hide under the front porch for an hour.
- Thank you for walking out on the porch (pretending to not know where I was hiding) and crying loud enough for me to hear I was missed.
- Thank you for welcoming me back home.
- Thank you for never running away from home—no matter how tempted *you* were.

Dear Mom, Thank You for Being Mine—*ask for it at your local bookstore.*